READ ON

Zig Zag

by Lada Josefa Kratky

NATIONAL GEOGRAPHIC

School Publishing

Do you want to see zigs and zags? Look for some.

She has a pot. Look at the
zigs and zags on the pot.

Mom wants a zig zag bag.
Do you see a bag with a zig
and a zag? You can look for
it here.

This rug has some zigs and zags. I like it. Do you?

Look here. Do you see the
zig and zag in this mat?

I can see some zigs and
zags here. Do you see the red
zig zag?

Look at me! I have a zig zag. Do you see it?